A is for the arrow

The arrow
hit the target

B

is for the binoculars

I took my binoculars into the woods
to try and get a closer look

C is for the crossbow

I enjoy hunting
with my crossbow

D is for the decoy

I like to use duck decoys
while hunting

 is for the elk

The elk bugles very loud

F

is for the firearm

We use firearms to hunt with

is for the GPS

The GPS helps me find where I am on the map

H is for the hunting

We enjoy hunting different animals throughout the year

I is for the iron sights

We use iron sights to aim our firearms

is for the jacket

We use our hunting jacket to stay warm

is for the knife

We use a knife to process animals

L

is for the license

HUNTING LICENSE

John Hunter
CID : #0216765421

We must have a hunting license to be able to hunt

is for the map

Maps help us from getting
lost in the woods

is for the night vision goggles

We use night vision goggles
to see in the dark

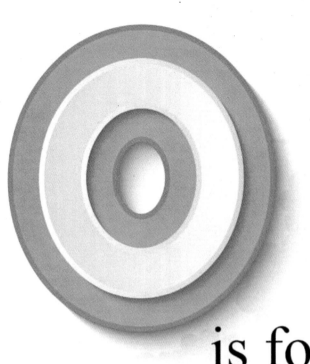 is for the orange hat

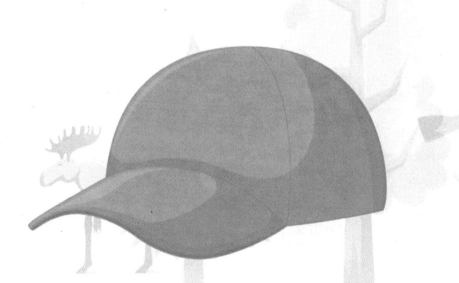

We must wear an orange hat to keep us safe while we hunt

P

is for the predator

We predator hunt to help
more animals survive

Q is for the quiver

A quiver holds our arrows

 is for the rangefinder

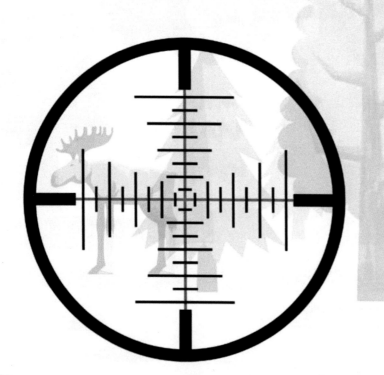

A rangefinder tells us how far away animals are

S

is for the shotgun

A shotgun fires lots of BBs

T is for the trail camera

Trail cameras show
us what animals are
in the area

U

is for the umbrella

Umbrellas keep us dry
when it is raining while
hunting

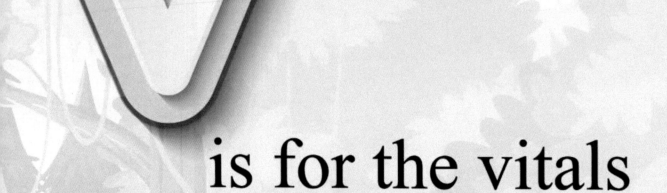

is for the vitals

We always aim for the vitals

is for the walkie talkies

Walkie talkies helps us
speak to other people

is for the X marks spot on map

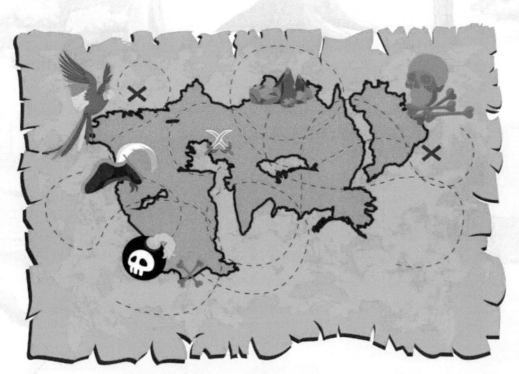

X marks the spot, so let's go and hunt

Y is for the yearling

A yearling is a young animal

Z

is for the zoom

We use the zoom
to see farther

Made in United States
Orlando, FL
26 February 2024

44123184R00015